Get Out of Own Way... and Get On With It

A Practical Guide to Stop Self-Judgment and Negative Thinking

Get Out of Your Own Way... and Get On With It

A Practical Guide to Stop Self-Judgment and Negative Thinking

By Peter E. Heymann

Kara—
Here's to a year
of Break-Throughs!

Peter Heyman

ISBN: 978-1-945446-09-2

www.BabypiePublishing.com

Acknowledgments

Earth who gave us all this food
Sun who made it ripe and good
Dearest Earth and dearest sun
We'll not forget what you have done.

This is the wonderful little salutation my family — Lois, Isaac, Gabriel, and I — say at mealtimes. It came to us from the school that my children attended in the Hudson Valley area of New York. The school is called Green Meadow and is part of the worldwide Waldorf education movement.

I'm reminded of this simple giving-of-thanks verse as I think about acknowledging the people and groups that influenced me to write *Get Out of Your Own Way . . . and Get On With It.*

A deep thank you to my life partner, Lois Kam Heymann, who for years has led me — sometimes scratching and pulling — to be open to both spiritual teachings and to my inner self. Thanks to our sons, Isaac and Gabriel, who gave me the opportunity to raise myself anew. In deeply involving myself in their growth and childhood development, I was able to fill the voids and hurts left from my own childhood. Through them I learned to feel, to know what *in the moment* means, and to be joyful.

Thanks to Hap Dunne and Andy Adkins, my early partners in running a youth program in New Canaan, Connecticut, in the early 1970s, and to all the kids we worked with. You inspired me to connect and communicate.

I'm grateful to the amazing people at Volunteer Counseling Services (VCS), Inc. in New City, New York, who trained me to be a volunteer counselor for twelve years and also trained me in anti-oppression community organizing work.

I also owe a huge thanks to Maura Leon. She generously coached me for more than a year, helping me get out of my own way so I could realize my dream of fifteen years and become a life coach.

I give acknowledgment and thanks to Landmark Worldwide, a powerful program all about personal change. The Landmark experience is amazing and can be truly transformational. Landmark provides tools for living and clearing the way for substantive change.

I appreciate my parents, who did everything they could for us. I wish I could have shared with them what I've learned about life and patterns of behavior. I know Esther and Al Heymann did the best they could, and I am sorry they weren't able to learn to *get out of their own way* and reach their full potential.

I feel so fortunate to have been able to grow and share insights with my brother Don. We have both devoted ourselves to changing family patterns and raising the next generation of Heymann boys to live up to their possibilities. And I am grateful to my older brother, Rick, who unfortunately passed away at age thirty. He taught me the invaluable lesson of empathy.

Finally, I acknowledge my colleagues in community organizing and social justice work. Organizing together, we have learned to break down walls of separation and stand together for equality and justice for all — with no exceptions.

Here's to connection, change, and positive transformation!

Table of Contents

CHAPTER TEN

Introduction

We all start life as babies filled with all possibilities and wonder. Then life happens; our unique circumstances and the people around us shape and affect us. We're a combination of everything and everyone we ever experience in life, although some people — parents, guardians, primary caregivers — clearly have a greater impact on us than others.

You didn't choose the parents or family you were born into. You didn't choose the environment you were born into, nor did you choose your wealth, class, race, ethnicity, culture, geography, housing, health, or family history. And you certainly didn't choose the circumstances and events that affected you in your formative years.

Make no mistake about it: life doesn't come with instructions. Every family faces challenges. Every person has difficulties. It's the early life challenges that shape and guide you toward your ways of being.

How did you get to be who you are today?

Understanding how you were guided to be who you are is critical to unlocking your full potential. If you can figure out this puzzle, you can choose the way you want to be moving forward. You can then, finally, exercise Free Will to *select* your ways of being and become the person you were always meant to be.

It is the challenges that you experience early in life that teach you how to navigate through your life, creating learned patterns of behavior. If you never look deeply into the patterns and circumstances that guided you to your ways of being, you will likely live out these repeating patterns in your relationships and careers.

When you live exclusively through these learned patterns of behavior you tend to form habits of being that can get in your way of changing and growing into the life you want. You will have difficulty finding your purpose or what will bring you joy in life if you remain trapped by life circumstances.

Get Out of Your Own Way . . . and Get On With It is designed to help people who are seeking positive change in their lives.

My purpose for writing this book is to share straightforward ways for discovering the key life patterns that guide and form our habits or ways of being. Once you see how you were guided to be, you can begin to establish new ways of being and unleash your potential.

I learned firsthand over the years, from various forms of counseling, coaching and personal growth group work, that substantive change is possible. It's never too late to learn and explore new ways of being. But it takes more than shining a light and looking at the ways we learned to be. It takes practicing new habits and new ways of being. The tools presented in this book are designed to help people understand their unique patterns and stories in order to clear the path for positive change.

It has been a joy to write this book of support using my experience with the tools and techniques of counseling and coaching. I have witnessed these tools help real people make real, substantive transformations. And I've practiced the techniques myself to transform my own life.

People from all walks of life share the same basic human needs and desires, though our life circumstances vary. While we all experience our own unique childhood dramas, there are, in addition, societal patterns of oppression that target particular groups of people. Racism, classism, sexism and other kinds of oppression are major causes of drama and trauma in some people's lives, especially people in marginalized groups.

Social change, social justice, and community organizing are necessary to change societal patterns of oppression. There are powerful movements in place and new ones are continually forming to tackle societal and institutional change.

However, it is important to recognize that individuals can change and transform *their own lives* substantially. Each individual can work on and change their patterns of behavior into new and more constructive ways of being. *Get Out of Your Own Way . . . and Get On With It* focuses on this kind of individual change and transformation.

So, let's get out of our own way . . . and get on with it!

Is Coaching Right for You?

Is life coaching for you?

Ask yourself these questions:

Would I like to express my feelings more effectively?

Would I like to know myself better?

Do I wish I could be happier than I am?

Am I struggling with procrastination and making decisions?

Would I like to know that I have options?

Am I seeking closer relationships?

Do I have the career I want?

Do I feel I'm blocked from living the life I want?

If you answered Yes to any or several of these questions, then coaching may be the way to break through.

CHAPTER ONE

Drama and Trauma
in Our Lives

DRAMA AND TRAUMA

I believe that every person, no matter how happy they seem, has experienced either drama or trauma in their upbringing. These experiences are powerful forces in our formative years.

Trauma refers to events or circumstances more serious than drama; being raised by an alcoholic or drug-abusing parent; being a victim of sexual or physical abuse; experiencing a tragic loss early in one's childhood. Traumatic circumstances are serious enough to put a child's life or well-being at risk. Not every life has *trauma*, but it is my feeling that every life does have *drama*.

Drama refers to repetitive nontraumatic events that cause a child to alter their natural patterns of behavior. The kind of drama and the impact of the events are different for every family, and for every child within that family. Drama can vary even among brothers and sisters within the same family because they experience things from a different point of view, and at a different point in time.

During child development, these repeating dramas or traumas go a long way toward establishing who we are, particularly how we learn to act and react. It is in navigating through the difficult events of our childhoods that we learn ways of being. These events mold or guide us to be, to act, and to feel certain ways; we learn to behave in certain ways to ease our paths, navigate through difficulties, or, in extremely traumatic circumstances, to survive.

Even the most perfect-looking family has drama to cope with because, very simply, life is dramatic. When living in any kind of community environment, we impact each other in many different ways. Life happens. The unexpected happens. We have to deal with problems that crop up in life, even with the best of intentions or best-laid plans.

In a family household, where a small group of people are together, day by day, there tend to be repeating patterns. For children, who often are extremely limited in their choice of relationships, exposure to the same people all day long ensures a consistency of stimuli. Repeating drama establishes our ways of being. Often, these ways can cause us difficulty in the long term.

EXPLORING PATTERNS OF BEHAVIOR

Do you ever find yourself walking through life feeling *stuck*?

It happens to most of us. Some of that feeling stuck is being, I think, trapped by this way that we learned to be and not to be. We don't have to stay there. We can get beyond that. We can look at it, we can see it for what it was, and put it in the past. Helping clients to explore and alter these patterns of behavior is what I try to do in a coaching situation. You will learn about my methods and philosophy in this book.

In general, my approach to coaching involves first looking at the past and asking important questions:

What drama did you experience?

What trauma did you experience?

How did you learn to be, to navigate, or survive the drama or trauma?

In order to navigate or survive, what strengths have you developed along the way?

What important elements of yourself have you abandoned along the way?

Are there any that you want to recapture?

It is important to note that our challenges often inspire us to develop *Strong Suits* — valuable ways of being that helped us navigate or survive. In coaching, we learn to celebrate those Strong Suits and rejoice in them; they are what helped us get to this point in life.

Just as you've learned ways of being, you've also learned how to *not* be certain ways. You've learned to drop certain things from your nature or from your personality, or from your ways of relating to the world, in order to navigate or survive. Part of coaching is to take a look and see what you've given up, so you can add any traits back into your ways of being.

Coaching, from my perspective and my approach, is different from therapy or counseling. Sometimes the distinction is a fine line, but there are differences. One of those differences has to do with how the process relates to history, or the past. In therapy and counseling, there tends to be more dwelling on the past, looking at events in great depth. A long period of time is spent sifting through what has happened in the past, and that's fine. I believe in counseling, and I believe in therapy for some people, even for most people.

But coaching is a little different. We look at the past simply to set a context for what's going on now, as a way of understanding what has happened to us and how we have learned to be.

As a coach, it is important to help people realize that those dramas and traumas happened a long time ago; they're not happening today so we don't need to carry them with us. The tendency in many people — even most people — is to carry that drama or trauma along with us as we mature and grow older, even after we leave the house and start our own families. We have a tendency to take our history with us, and along with it, the drama and trauma.

That's why I say that coaching is more about today and tomorrow, rather than staying in the past. We look at the past to see the context, to learn our Strong Suits, to identify the drama or trauma, to label it for what it was, to see it clearly, but leave it in the past. What happened isn't happening today. It happened long ago.

If you can look at it in this context, it can be easier to put the past where it belongs, and to clear the way for living life the way you want to, in a full, complete, balanced way. You can't do that until you really take a look at these dramas and traumas, and how you learned to navigate through your life, how you learned to be. That's a big part of the coaching experience — a critical part — because you can't really move forward freely until you do that.

ONE FAMILY DRAMA

I know a great deal about these issues from my own personal experience, and I'll take a couple of moments to share. I often use my own experience in my coaching sessions as a way to illustrate what I mean by drama and trauma.

I was raised in the 1950s and '60s in northern New Jersey, and from the outside looking in, my family life appeared idyllic.

My mother and father lived together in a nice home and raised three boys. Father was the breadwinner, Mother was a stay-at-home mom. Our family image looked like those of the old TV shows, like *My Three Sons* or *Father Knows Best*. But even in this classic, white, middle-class family in the northeastern part of New Jersey, there was plenty of drama that other people couldn't see. My brothers and I certainly experienced our share.

My older brother Rick was born with a congenital heart condition, a serious condition. I don't even remember the name of it, but I do remember that his heart was literally on the wrong side of his chest cavity. He also had holes in his heart and other serious health issues. This certainly was a drama that strongly affected his life, as well as the lives of the rest of the family.

I was born about two and a half years after Rick, and the first stories I remember hearing about myself were set in the birthing room. My mother used to tell the story about how when I was born, the doctor or the nurse held me up as they do — to check fingers, toes, and vital signs — and presented me to my mother with the words:

"Here's your healthy son."

My mother, as she repeated that story — and I heard it often — over the years, translated that message from the doctor as:

"This one's *perfect.*"

Right from the very beginning, then, I had the responsibility to be perfect, and that continued through my early years. I was the son who was perfect, and so, I felt pressured to be that way. Moreover, my brother's health issues and my parents' fears about them strongly affected me as we were growing up.

Siblings need to mix it up. They need to tease each other. They need to fight. They need to experiment with each other, have fun with each other, and freely play and push boundaries together. We weren't allowed to do that in our house.

When I picture my brother Rick, I always picture my mother behind him. This was a repeating image I had from about age five. We'd be arguing or I'd be teasing my brother, and my mother would be in pantomime behind him, waving her arms to make me stop. She would pat her chest with an expression that only mothers can have, communicating without talking. The message was:

Pete, stop! Be careful. You're hurting him. Don't hurt Rick.

For me, this was a repeating drama that deeply affected me. To navigate that drama, I developed several traits. I learned to be independent, and I learned to be strong. Whether my mother intended it or not, the message that I received was that my feelings would hurt my brother. Over time, with the message repeated constantly, it developed into a fear that my feelings could actually *kill* my brother.

A little boy who wants to live a free, fun life doesn't want to take part in that kind of restriction, so I hightailed it out of the house each morning. We lived near a park and it was really beautiful, so I went down to the park, and mixed it up with the kids in the neighborhood. I learned sports, I learned to be an athlete, and I learned to relate freely and have fun outside of the house. I never did come home until the six o'clock whistle. That's how I lived my life. I really didn't relate to my brother very much because I didn't want to be restricted.

My particular life experiences impacted the development of my ways of being, as you can see.

So what Strong Suits did I develop from these experiences?

As a child, I learned to be strong, I learned to be independent, and I learned to be very careful. That's what helped me get to this point in my life, and it's what helped me be me.

I think everybody would agree that being independent, strong, and careful are positive qualities. The problem for me — and for many people — is, in addition to learning how to be, we also learn how *not* to be. We learn how to drop things from our nature, or from our way of life that's really true to our core or who we are.

What did I learn *not* to be?

I learned not to be spontaneous and not to fully express my feelings. I learned not to even *feel* needs or wants, and certainly not to express needs or wants. All through my life, then, there was a part of me that wasn't complete.

I'm sorry to say that this incompleteness lasted into my fifties. It wasn't until I finally faced the dynamics of my Strong Suits and what I gave up to navigate my drama that I realized what of myself I had lost.

I used to walk around with this strong mythology about myself that I don't need people. I am fortunate to have a loving wife of forty years and two dynamic, terrific sons, but I felt I didn't need anybody else.

I had acquaintances, and was certainly social, but I walked around thinking: *I don't need anybody. I don't need anybody.*

Once I looked at the dynamics of what formed me, through the drama that I described, I realized — no, I wasn't being my true self. Actually, when I got in better touch with my feelings, I saw the opposite is true. I really need connections with people. I really need to express my feelings. I have a *strong* need for that, which I didn't face for most of my life.

Now, I can reclaim that part of myself, because I can put the past in the past by facing it, by talking about it, and by processing it. I can add those qualities that were missing, and lead a more complete, full, and balanced life.

This is the philosophy that I use in my coaching. I think it's beneficial to go through this process of identifying the drama or trauma in your life, and how you learned to be who you are — as a way of clearing the way to leading the life that you want.

I don't care what age you are. I don't care if you're a teenager. I don't care if you're in your twenties, thirties, or forties. I don't care if you're seventy years old or older. I've grown to know this process well. I've seen it work, and it can benefit everyone.

In the ensuing chapters, we'll be talking more about this process. You'll see how you can start by facing the drama or trauma that was repeating in your early years, learn to understand how it has impacted who you are, and learn how to move forward and transform your life.

You can start living a life that's truer to your core being.

You can live a life that you love.

What Drama or Trauma Shaped Your Early Life?

Make a list of the drama and trauma that affected your life in ages three through eight, nine through twelve, and into your high school years.

Write the Drama or Trauma you experienced at three important stages of your life:

Ages 3–8 _____

_____

_____

Ages 9–12 _____

_____

_____

High School Years _____

_____

_____

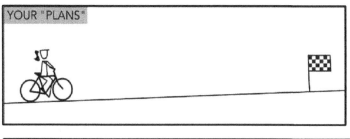

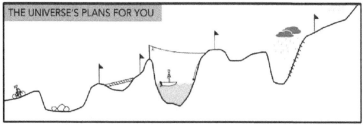

Reprinted with permission from DogHouseDiaries.com

CHAPTER TWO

How We Learn To Be

When you change the way you look at things . . .
the things you look at change.
~ Dr. Wayne Dyer
The Power of Intention

WAYS WE LEARN TO BE

Before you can make changes in your life, you must take a close look at yourself. You need to understand how you learned to be who you are. This is an extremely important facet of coaching. Remember what Shakespeare wrote so many years ago. In *Hamlet,* he gave us the key question of all time:

"To be or not to be, that is the question . . ."

Let's take a look at the ways we learn to be—and not to be.

We learn to be certain ways because of the experiences that we have in life. In fact, we're all a function of everything we've experienced up until this point, including every person we've met and every interaction we've ever had. They make us who we are.

For children, it is the critically important primary caretakers—parents, guardians and other caregivers—who have the biggest role in determining how we learn to be, or not to be. Also important to consider is the next level of relationships for children—school and social environments—that are important from early years into high school years.

We are molded by the people, the environment, the drama, and trauma; everything we've been exposed to and every experience that we've had.

I often think of this concept in terms of an equation. On the left side of the equal sign is everything that contributed to forming us, and on the right side is who we are today. No matter what age we are, we're all a combination of our biology, chemistry, and genetics, plus all the things that happened to us, including the drama or trauma in our formative years, from birth through age eighteen or so.

How we act and react—who we are in the world—is the sum total of all of those elements.

NATURE VERSUS NURTURE

Considering this idea brings up the philosophical argument of *nature versus nurture*. You can see that I included elements of both schools of thought in my description of what contributes to forming us. In my coaching practice I am more focused on the influences of our experiences (the *nurture* category) on our behavior, but biology (the *nature* category) is part of who we are as well.

Which is more significant?

There really is no clear answer to that question, but it's my sense that they are both significant. It is a combination of nature and nurture together that results in the ways of being that we learn to be or not to be. We can be sure, however, that, for either category—nature or nurture—in our early lives, very little of our environment was a matter of choice.

How much of your early life was a matter of choice?

Pull the camera back a little bit and look at your life from a wider perspective. You didn't choose the parents that you were born to, or the primary caregivers you ended up with. You didn't choose the environment that you were raised in. You didn't choose the wealth of your parents or the status that you were born to. You didn't choose the race that you were born into or your ethnicity. You didn't choose any of those environmental factors at all. That's the happenstance of birth and life.

This leads us to an important question:

If you agree, as I do, that all of these factors make us who we are, do we actually have any choices at all?

If it's all a happenstance or accident of birth and circumstance, what about Free Will?

If it's true that we are the sum of everything and everyone we've ever experienced, not much of that involved Free Will, did it?

Don't we have Free Will?

This is a philosophical argument that keeps freshmen and sophomores up in all-night talk sessions. It's my contention that we *have* Free Will, but many of us don't *exercise* it. You cannot use Free Will until you understand the circumstances that led you to who you are today.

Why is that?

Your patterns of behavior have been established by the circumstances that led you here. They become automatic responses that have been programmed by coping mechanisms. Making purposeful choices can only be possible when you understand your tendencies and the reasons for them. Once you take a good look at yourself, and understand how you got where you are, that's when Free Will can finally kick in.

TRAITS WE GIVE UP — LEARNING TO MAKE CHOICES

Coaching can help with this personal growth journey. When you can take a look at your life and see all of your early experiences and understand what has led to the ways that you've learned to be and not be, you can start on the road to genuine freedom. You can make behavioral choices instead of automatically reacting to situations.

In addition, when you identify what you have lost in your nature along the way, you can take back some control, harness your Free Will, and say:

Okay, I gave up certain parts of my natural way of being as a child in order to navigate certain circumstances. Now as an adult, if I see that, I can choose to add that back into my life.

For example, in my personal life, I gave up my spontaneity, and my openness with my emotions due to a repeating drama in my family. I learned to adopt a certain way of being, and also learned certain ways *not* to be.

Once I understood that, I could look at my life and *choose* to alter my patterns of behavior. I could say to myself:

Here is something I want to change. I want to be more open. I want to be more expressive of my feelings, my wants, and my needs. I want to reclaim my need for connection and closeness.

I could then practice and work toward that. That's where Free Will comes in. That's why it's really important to understand how we learned to be certain ways and how we learned not to be other ways.

Here is a more detailed example:

Imagine a young girl who was raised by alcoholic parents. In an alcoholic home, which is in my definition a traumatic situation, there were likely some erratic, emotional ups and downs for the child. That young girl would learn to be extremely aware of her surroundings, and incredibly intuitive so as to see explosive behavior before it even develops, to learn how to navigate and work around it.

A child like that would likely learn to be mature beyond her years, because she would have to learn to take care of situations in the family that, normally, a parent would take on. This little girl would learn to be responsible. She would likely become an excellent problem-solver after handling those ups and downs and erratic behaviors. She would also learn to be extremely careful. She might learn to be very private, to keep all of that dark behavior inside, so that other people—neighbors and family members outside of the immediate family—wouldn't see.

Those are all ways of learning how to be and not to be. The little girl's experiences would teach her how to navigate through a very difficult situation.

We all learn to navigate our young lives in this way, and some of us learn to survive serious traumas by adopting protective behavior. By identifying and assessing how *your* ways of being developed, you can get a good understanding of yourself and your current behavior patterns.

You can identify those patterns that are your Strong Suits and see that they're important to hold onto. They have helped you become the person that you are right now. Strong Suits are like muscles we develop to help us survive difficulty and we need to celebrate them. We will discuss in detail in the next chapter.

Once you have the choice to act with Free Will, you will certainly want to keep your Strong Suits, but there may be other qualities or patterns you will want to change. In addition, as we've discussed, you will want to identify any qualities you lost or gave up along the way that you now want to reclaim.

The little girl in our example had to learn to give up certain things; it is likely she became guarded, and lost the ability to trust and connect to others because of her immediate environment. Once she is able to see these things as an adult, she can decide to work on regaining some lost qualities and abilities. She can work on becoming more trusting and more connected to others. This is a true, positive use of Free Will.

It is only after identifying our unique patterns of behavior and the forces that created them that we can freely choose our own paths.

How Did You Learn To Be?

Write the ways you learned to be. As you write, consider these questions:

- How did you learn to be this way?

- Who taught you to be this way?

- When did you learn to be this way?

CHAPTER THREE

Celebrate Your Strong Suits

EXPLORING YOUR STRONG SUITS

Your Strong Suits are wonderful—they are how you got through your early life up to today. Celebrate them. You want to know them, honor them, and embrace them. You don't want to discard your Strong Suits; instead, you want to build on them.

Getting to know your Strong Suits can be a joyful part of gaining understanding of who you are. It can help you build your self-esteem to explore the positive traits that got you through to where you are today. And they can be building blocks for ways you choose to be in your future.

As we've already discussed, Strong Suits are valuable ways of being that helped you navigate or survive the unique circumstances of your growing years. We all learn to develop traits that help us navigate the early drama, or survive the early trauma in our lives. They are traits that you want to highlight and emphasize in yourself because they are useful skills that can be applied to other areas of life. Strong Suits are positive and powerful. They got us through from point A to point B and now can function to help us move forward in our lives.

DEVELOPMENT OF STRONG SUITS UNDER PRESSURE

Unique Strong Suits develop under the pressure of particular dramas and traumas. Some examples follow.

Example 1: Abandonment

Abandonment by a primary caregiver at an early age can lead to the development of the Strong Suits of independence, strength, and caution. The child may also learn to be keenly aware of his surroundings and the people around him. These Strong Suits would function to protect the child and help him navigate and even survive the issues of abandonment.

Would these characteristics be beneficial to an adult?

Certainly independence, strength, and caution could be excellent qualities for an adult. Although they may have developed under circumstances that were undesirable, they are, nonetheless, valuable skills that would be useful both in personal life and the workplace for many careers.

Example 2: Baby of the Family

A boy who was born the youngest of three sons may be overprotected and even babied. He might learn to smile and be endearing as his way of navigating through his family life to gain attention and recognition. In trying to be heard over the other children, he might learn some strong and creative communication skills. He might develop strong listening skills to know when and where he can jump in and be part of the family discourse and communication.

Creativity and communication might become his Strong Suits. These would be excellent skills for a teacher or counselor and would be valuable for all kinds of person-to-person interactions in life.

Example 3: Irresponsible Caregiver

A child raised in a household in which the primary caregiver was unreliable or erratic, perhaps due to mental illness or drug abuse, might learn to be an analytical problem solver. This Strong Suit would serve her well during her childhood and might help her throughout her life. Becoming skilled at analyzing and problem solving would be a great advantage in a science career, or in architecture or engineering.

Example 4: Pressure to Perform

Someone who faces an ongoing drama due to a judgmental mother who constantly pressures her to work may develop the powerful Strong Suits of responsibility, a work ethic, independence, resiliency, problem-solving, diligence, taking direction, and managing tasks to completion.

As an adult, these skills might make her an expert in goal-setting and management; these are skills that would be of great value in running an entrepreneurial business venture and would be useful in many other areas of life.

No matter how your Strong Suits developed, you need to acknowledge, honor, and celebrate them. It is our Strong Suits that can take us to our next level of purpose and achievement if we honor and celebrate them. We can build on our Strong Suits and use them to lead the life we want and love.

If we can *add* to our Strong Suits and modify ourselves to be more balanced and truer to our early nature and possibilities, we could really shake up our lives and flourish.

That's where analyzing our drama or trauma and ways we learned to be and not to be can play a very powerful role in creating our future.

THE FLIP SIDE OF STRONG SUITS

As you might already suspect, our Strong Suits can also bring with them some negative elements — ways of reacting that are not constructive and may prevent us from happiness.

Example 5: Judgmental Parents

A girl born to highly judgmental parents who treated her as the star of the family but also passed judgment about everything she wore and how she looked and carried herself gained Strong Suits as well. The drama guided her to be a strong personality, to be careful about her image and appearance, to shine in public, to perform and provide energy in a room, and to bring emotion and excitement to her relationships.

You can see that these Strong Suits have value, but can you see that they might present some challenges for her as well?

It is important to look carefully at your Strong Suits and see what is positive and valuable, but also identify the challenges they present. For example, the Strong Suits described in this example allowed the young woman to shine, but in learning to perform for others, she may also have lost some of herself. She may make a point of pleasing others to the extent that she does not know what she, herself, wants. This could easily lead to a life of trying to please others and sometimes not knowing how to please herself.

Everyone develops Strong Suits to navigate or survive drama and trauma. It is critical to assess and understand what your

Strong Suits are and why you developed them. Remember, it is only after exploration and analysis of what we learned *to be* and *not to be* that we can exercise Free Will. Until we do this exploration, our actions are just automatic responses to situations that were designed by our early life training.

Once we understand this dynamic in our lives we can then knowingly elect to *be* and *not be* the way we want. We can choose to add back to our lives the traits we had to give up in order to navigate or survive. We can become our true, full selves.

The girl in our story can get away from reacting to her parents' expectations and instead, get in touch with her own desires and wants.

She can begin to ask herself:

How do I want to look and behave?

What is my purpose and what will bring me joy?

It takes practice, for sure. We can't snap our fingers and change ways of being that were ingrained for years or even decades. But change we can. It takes awareness and desire — and practice, practice, practice.

Celebrate your Strong Suits. By definition they are very positive attributes that helped get you to this point in life and can keep moving you forward.

Conversely, we also need to identify, assess, and explore what we learned *not to be* in order to navigate and survive to this point in life, and we will learn more about that in the next chapter.

Once you distinguish what happened in the past from your present-day life, you can put the past in the past and move on to the future you want to create for yourself. You can recognize that all the difficult things of the past did happen. But they are the past.

We all need to put the past in the past and from that space, create possibilities for our future. We can create the Ways of Being we want for ourselves. The possibilities are exciting and meaningful. Free Will can reign.

What Are Your Strong Suits?

- List your Strong Suits

- Appreciate them

- Celebrate them

Your Strong Suites got you to today.

CHAPTER FOUR

What You Gave Up To Be

WHAT DID YOU GIVE UP?

In the last chapter, the child who was abandoned emotionally in early childhood gave up his innate ability to trust people. This would likely result in a pattern of distrustful behavior as an adult. But it is possible for him to reclaim the ways of being he had to give up.

He can learn to ask, "What do I *want*?"

And so can you.

We've been talking about the effects of drama and trauma in our lives, how they help to guide us, how they dictate the ways that we learn to be to navigate the drama or survive the trauma. The flip side to that, or the corollary to that, is that the drama and trauma in our early lives also guide us in ways *not* to be. We all give up some of our natural traits and tendencies when we are very young.

Often we need to give up part of ourselves—or our ways of being—in order to navigate or survive the drama or trauma. It is vital to look at these lost elements of ourselves. When we are trying to take a look at who we are, where we're going, what we want, or what our true purpose is, it is important to assess not only how we've learned to be, but how we learned *not* to be; what we gave up along the way.

Everybody's story is different, of course, because everybody is different. Everybody has different dramas or traumas. It's the repetitive dramatic or traumatic events in our early years that really tend to dictate how we form ourselves, and how we learn how to be and how not to be.

LOST WAYS AND HOW THEY IMPACT OUR LIVES

Below are some examples of how this kind of loss may manifest itself. They are from people that I've coached and other people that I've known. I will use myself as an example as well.

Example 1: Giving Up Laughter and Celebration

There was a woman who had grown up with a well-meaning mother. The mother cared for her little girl, but the mother was also pretty harsh in her treatment of this little girl. Mom was a very demanding taskmaster; this little girl was raised with to-do lists — every day, a list of things to do: tasks, chores, and responsibilities that were quite specific.

Every day, she learned that she needed to attend to that to-do list, and if she didn't, there would be a price to pay. That was the drama in her life, this rather severe, strict list of things to do. In keeping with what we talked about previously, from that drama, she learned how to avoid the wrath of her mother by attending to the daily to-do list and by being extremely responsible.

She took on the Strong Suits of being super responsible, dutiful, loyal, and very purposeful in her young life, and learned to be quite mature beyond her years in attending to all of this responsibility. Being purposeful, responsible, mature, and serious — I think everyone would agree — are very positive traits to develop in one's life. However, she also learned how *not to be* in order to satisfy her mother's very strong, ongoing, severe demands.

She lost a certain amount of her joy, her spontaneity, her playfulness, and her laughter, and she lost the quality of being a carefree girl having fun in life. She gave up a lot in order to attend to this to-do list of responsibilities.

She carried that drama with her over the years. As a young woman, a mature woman, and later a middle-aged woman, she also carried that purposefulness, responsibility, maturity, and that strong work ethic with her into adulthood. That's not a bad thing, because she's a very responsible person, and that has paid off for her. She's achieved quite a bit in her life.

However, in our talks and an examination of this dramatic portion of her life, she learned to take a look at what she gave up. She found there were some qualities she wanted to work on recovering and recapturing in her life. She wanted to learn again to be free-flowing and spontaneous, more joyful, more emotional, more playful, and to have more humor in her life. She happens to be a very funny person, but she had learned to curtail her humor because her responsibilities were the priority. Her Strong Suits always led the way.

Now she's able to practice another way of being, or perhaps a way to *add* to the way she's learned to be. She doesn't want to give up being responsible. She doesn't want to give up being purposeful and mature, but wants to add to that some joy and spontaneity.

She also wanted to be able to celebrate her achievements. When she was growing up, not only did she have to attend to this list very strictly and achieve everything, otherwise her mother would get very, very angry and punish her, but she also had to learn to do these things without any celebration of having achieved anything. Her mother was there to criticize, but not there to rejoice in her achievement.

In a rather severe way, she learned to be very humble. Again, there's nothing wrong with being humble, but you want to be balanced in life. You want to be able to enjoy what you have achieved without gloating or bragging, but to be able to celebrate it. She's working on gaining the ability to do this. It takes work to undo what you have learned by years of practice.

Example 2: Giving Up Expression of Feelings and Spontaneity

As I talked with a man in his early forties, he was able to identify his childhood issues and some of the consequences of them. He was raised by a mother who was very erratic. Likely, from what he says, she may have been bipolar. She was highly emotional and also was very stern. She could fly off the handle at any moment in fits of rage and anger. In addition, he had a father in the household who was rather distant.

Think about what it must have been like for a young boy to live in this household.

From these early experiences he learned some valuable Strong Suits. A child who is raised by a parent who has severe ups and downs in a bipolar fashion and can explode at any moment commonly develops a keenly aware sense of what's around him, and this boy was no different. He learned how to be very intuitive so that he could anticipate his mother's feelings and reactions well before she began to express them. He also learned to be very independent, because he couldn't count on his mother for much calm guidance. And he learned to spend time on his own because he wanted to avoid the wrath of his mother.

Self-reliance, independence, intuition, and a high sense of awareness of what's around him—these became his Strong Suits. Eventually, from that high sense of awareness and intuition, he also developed exceptional problem-solving skills. He could anticipate problems before they even happened. Later in life, that would prove very valuable to him in his profession.

Of course, in addition to learning how to be, and the Strong Suits that he developed to navigate his situation, he also learned how *not* to be. Similarly to that little girl we just discussed, he learned to give up lightness, fun, joy, free expression of his feelings, and spontaneity that he had as a young boy, but had to curtail, keep inside, and deny.

Now, as a grown man with responsibilities—a child of his own, a business to run—he is learning to take a look at these factors in his life, these ways of being and not being that he learned, so that he can choose how he wants to be as a man, as a father, and as an owner and a manager in his business.

He's practicing and learning to take a look at all of those qualities he learned to give up as a child, figuring out how to add them back into his life. He's also celebrating his Strong Suits, because they have made him a master craftsman in his field. He's a real problem-solver in his work, but now he's also learning to walk a little more lightly, and enjoy himself. He's getting more and more in touch with the feelings that he gave up as a young boy.

Example 3: Giving Up Trust

The third story is an all too common story. It's about a young girl who was raised by alcoholic parents. Both parents were alcoholics. In addition to that, her mother was also extremely judgmental and demanding. The father was more erratic, yet did provide her affection in a secretive, just-between-the-two-of-them way. He had his own way of acknowledging her specialness, and showing her some love.

In my experience, children with parents who are either alcohol or drug abusers commonly develop a highly tuned, keen sense of attentiveness. They are excellent listeners and are intuitive. These skills enable them to anticipate needs and difficulties in their world.

The home life of a child being raised by an alcoholic parent—or two of them, in this case—has a lot of turmoil, ups and downs, and requires children to cope with erratic behavior. Those children really need to be highly intuitive and very keenly aware of what's going on. These were some of the skills that this girl cultivated in her young life.

As she was growing up, this young girl also developed creativity. This Strong Suit that she forged was for the purpose of occupying and comforting herself. She learned how to write; she learned how to create fantasies and stories. This was the way she both soothed and excited herself; with imaginative stories that she could create at any time. She became a writer at a very young age, and continued into adulthood.

In her case, the Strong Suit she developed really paid off in her life, because she went into the writing profession.

In addition, seeking adventure and new places became vitally important to her as she grew up. It was the way she not only got away from the erratic behavior of alcoholic parents, but got away from her very demanding, judgmental mother. As an adult, this developed into a strong lust for travel. When she was traveling, she could just be herself.

Between her creativity and her writing, she created a world she could escape to, and when she got older and could venture out, she traveled the world.

Her Strong Suits, cultivated under the pressure of her home life, served her well and gave her a profession in which she could excel. But she also gave up something really basic in order to survive the trauma of being raised by alcoholic parents. She gave up her sense of trust as a young child. She learned she couldn't trust people because of her erratic home environment.

She had a very strong-willed mother who taught her—not purposely, but just in her actions and the way she related to her daughter—not to trust other people, and to be distrustful of other people. As a child, she was repeatedly told by her mother that nobody could be counted on *except* her mother. That was something that this young girl learned well, and it carried through into her life as an adult. She gave up trust.

Now as a woman in her early forties, facing the rest of her life, she is taking a good, hard look at the drama and trauma in her life, and how she learned to be and not be. She is now beginning to especially work on that area of trust. In our discussions, we talk about how important trust is in *any* relationship. As you might imagine, this woman has had difficulties in her relationships with men over the years. A lot of her problems came down to this central, core issue of trust.

Example 4: Giving Up Feelings and Desires

For the fourth example, I'll tell you a little more about my own childhood. As I related previously, I was raised by very overprotective parents. Not so much protective of me, but protective of my older brother, who was born with a congenital heart condition. That was a cloud of drama over my family; my parents related to my brother, first, and then when I came along about two and a half years later, it affected me and was the drama in my early life.

I was taught to be so careful with my older brother; so careful with my own feelings, desires, wants, and joys; I had to keep everything in, so as not to hurt my brother. As I mentioned before, I was taught to fear that my strong feelings — positive or negative feelings: anger, joy, celebration, anxiety, sadness — would hurt my brother, or even kill my brother.

On the positive side, I learned from that to be independent, strong, and very careful. Those are some of my Strong Suits that I've carried with me into adulthood. There's nothing wrong with them; they're what helped me navigate and get to the ripe old age that I am today. Those traits came to be very valuable to me in my life.

But what did I give up?

What I gave up were things like expressing my feelings freely, being emotional, even acknowledging that I have emotions, desires, wants, and needs. I was taught at a very early age, through actions, not to even express simple things that I wanted.

Even when it came to birthday gifts, if I wanted something particular, I never asked for it. I never asked for anything. I felt I wasn't allowed to ask. I remember as a high school varsity baseball player, I was playing center field and I was using a baseball glove that I had when I was in little league. Finally, it became dilapidated and unusable. Rather than simply ask my father or my mother for a baseball glove, I borrowed a friend's glove that he used when he was in Little League. It was too small, and it was old, and that's what I ended up playing with for two years on a varsity level!

I look back at that, and I just can't believe it.

How could I not even express the desire for a new baseball glove?

It's not that my parents didn't have the money. They did, and they would have gotten it in a flash. But I learned not to express what I wanted or needed, and it all linked back to the fear of hurting — even the fear of killing — my older brother.

Many people spend their adult lives without exploring how those early situations of drama and trauma have affected them. If you don't face them, you just carry them along with you. You continue to manage your life with your Strong Suits, but unless you dive a little more deeply and take a look at what happened in your early life, you won't see how you learned *not* to be.

WHEN YOUR PAST WON'T STAY THERE

Often at this point in the coaching process, when we start exploring loss, strong feelings will come up about the past. It is always difficult to understand — and this is true of the previous examples I talked about, too — that the dramas or traumas in our lives are things that happened, but they're finite and they have *ended.*

I can take a look at what happened — the repeating vision of my mother waving her arms and patting her chest so I knew to be careful with my brother — but it happened so long ago. It was me, as I grew up, who chose to carry it with me, along with the fear of expressing my feelings, as if it were part of the present instead of the past.

Carrying the past with me this way kept me from living a fuller, richer, more complete life along the way. But I'm happy to say I can do that now. We will talk more in depth about letting go of the past in Chapter Seven.

Discovering what we learned *not to be* can be particularly rewarding and helpful to our lives. That was definitely true for me, and I'm so thankful that — even though it took me a long time — I took a look at this in a clear and well-coached way. I saw what I gave up.

Now I am continually practicing being in touch with my feelings, expressing my feelings, and trusting that it's okay to express my wants and needs. It brings a lot of joy to me that I can do that and become a more complete person now. That's what this exercise of looking at how you learned to be and how you learned not to be can do for us.

It can really free us. I've experienced it myself and I've seen it in people I've coached.

Once you take a look at the drama and trauma in your life, and see how you learned to navigate them, how you learned to be and not to be, you can start to create the future that you want to create. You can add to the way you act and interact in this world. It's very freeing. It's amazingly freeing to no longer feel trapped by your past circumstances, your past drama or trauma.

A WORD ABOUT PARENTS

Have you noticed that all of our examples have much to do with the behavior of our parents?

It is true that childhood drama and trauma frequently are caused by our relationships with our parents, although it doesn't have to be so — sometime events that happen outside of the nuclear family can be important issues. When we are looking at parent behavior, however, it is important to look back from a healthy, empathetic perspective.

In this process, we are looking to identify the patterns that impacted our growth and made us react the way we do in life. We are not trying to point fingers and lay blame. We don't want to put energy into talking about bad parenting.

When I'm coaching, I emphasize that, most of the time, parents have done the best they could to give their children all that they had to give. They were probably constricted themselves by the drama and trauma that they were raised with when *they* were growing up. These things have a way of continuing across generations in some way, until you shine a metaphorical flashlight on the early experience of drama and trauma, and see how it affected you as an individual. It is possible that your efforts to improve your own life can help break dysfunctional family cycles. Gaining the ability to access Free Will in our lives can break us out of behavioral patterns that may have persisted for generations.

DETERMINISM AND THE QUESTION OF FREE WILL

Determinism is a way of looking at events in your life. It proposes the idea that all events are determined by specific causes. A deterministic view of what we've been discussing would be to say that who I am today is the result of the combination of all the events and experiences of my previous years.

I don't want to get into a lengthy philosophical discussion, but I think this concept is directly related to the current topic. I do subscribe to the idea of determinism. It tells us that we are, indeed, a collection of everything that happens to us, every experience and every relationship.

Certainly parenting and nuclear family relationships are primary, but we are a bundle of everything that we've ever experienced. Everything we've ever experienced has a way of guiding us to be a certain way in life. Certainly the drama and trauma that we've been talking about were major factors that determined how we learned to be and not to be.

That brings up a question: Do we have Free Will as human beings?

As has already been stated, it is my feeling that we have Free Will, but we really cannot exercise it until we take a look at the drama and trauma in our lives, see what happened for what it was, put it in its proper place, and understand the impact of these events on what we've come to be and not to be.

For example, now that I know how I learned to be in terms of my Strong Suits, and also what I gave up, I can say to myself:

Let me take a look at what I gave up. Let me take a look at spontaneity, free expression of feeling, emotion, desire, want, celebration, and joy.

I can then say: *Yeah, if I added some of that to my life, I would have a more balanced, fulfilled life. Let me figure out some ways to practice adding these things back into my life.*

That's when Free Will kicks in. That's when we can create possibilities for ourselves.

What You Gave Up To Be

What traits did you give up to navigate the drama or survive the trauma in your early life?

Write the ways you learned NOT TO BE in order to navigate the drama or survive the trauma.

These are the traits or Ways of Being you gave up in order to survive.

Think how your life would be if you didn't have to give up some of your Ways of Being.

CHAPTER FIVE

Stories and Myths

OUR STORIES

Our lives are all about a series of events and happenings, some mundane and some incredibly powerful, even life changing.

Some of what happened has had an immense impact. If events form part of a pattern in early life stages, what happened could have caused us to create a story—an interpretation of what happened to you and what it means—that we carry from the past to the present and into the future.

Whatever actually happened, happened. At some point it is over. Yet, if dramatic or traumatic, we tend to create a story around the events or circumstances to make sense of or assuage the dramatic happenings. It's those stories we create that we carry forward with us, instead of putting past happenings where they belong, in the past.

It is important to understand that the story you carry isn't just an objective tale of what happened to you; it is your interpretation of the meaning of what happened. The story is a private message you have created for yourself. It is often quite limiting. It is also difficult to let go of your story when you've held it for many years.

We tend to blame whoever perpetrated what happened, even if what happened stopped decades ago. We need to stop doing this. What happened, happened. It's over.

We are not responsible for what happened to us in our early life, but we are responsible for the stories or myths we create. We are responsible for carrying the stories with us into our future.

EXAMPLES OF STORIES AND MYTHS

Story 1: Tasks Without Joy

The first example is the young girl we began to discuss in the last chapter, whose life revolved around tasks and to-do lists.

Given daily to-do lists of chores from a young age, this child was expected to work diligently and complete every task. She was never praised or recognized for accomplishing her to-do list. Yet when she failed to complete any task on her list she was strongly chastised. This was a daily happening throughout her early childhood and into teenage years.

What story did she carry from this history?

The story she created around what happened was a story of responsibility, maturity, drudgery, seriousness, and humility. It could be summarized:

Life is only a series of responsibilities, tasks to complete without joy or celebration.

She carried this story into her future into her adulthood and into parenting her own children.

She had to learn to see this pattern of what happened (the continuous to-do lists, demands, and responsibilities) for what they were—things that happened, things that were imposed, but they are now over. No one today has the power over her that her mother had imposed. Once she could see what happened for what it was and that it had actually been over for decades, she could put it in the past and practice the freedom and joy of creating her own priorities and learning to celebrate her own accomplishments.

Story 2: Don't Feel and Don't Need

The second is my story. My mother, if you recall, constantly let me know to stifle my feelings so as not to hurt my brother. I learned to keep my feelings, my accomplishments completely to myself, never stating my own needs. I internalized this way of being to protect my brother's feelings so I wouldn't outshine him. For decades, my mother and father made me feel that my feelings, needs and accomplishments would make my brother feel bad, would hurt him.

The story I created around these happenings was this:

My feelings and accomplishments could actually kill my brother. I must keep them hidden inside.

It wasn't until my fifties that I finally learned that what happened in my young life growing up was over, and I could put it in the past and stop carrying it forward in my present and future.

I can now practice being spontaneous with my feelings and celebrating my joys and accomplishments. I know that the good things that happen to me won't hurt anyone, not even my brother.

Story 3: Better Off

I carried another myth with me as well. My father was distant, stern, and removed emotionally from me. My father was put on a pedestal by my mother as a perfect man and father, yet he was disconnected to me. And it came out that much of his distance was around protecting a long-time extramarital relationship.

When that all came out in the open in my late teens I created a myth that I was the one out of all his three sons who had it best because of this distance, that the distance and lack of connection with my father was a good thing and I was the lucky one. My myth was:

I am better off when I don't connect deeply with anyone.

I held this myth for years and years. Finally in open sharing with my younger brother I finally realized that no, this myth was just to protect myself from the pain of the emotional abandonment.

The light finally went off that I deeply missed closeness with my father. And that myth I created kept me from acknowledging my need to connect with people. The myth I carried all those years was powerful; it kept me distant and disconnected from people. I now have put that past in the past. I now see that within a core part of me is the need to connect deeply with others. I now have the freedom to redefine and live my core purpose of connection.

Story 4: Everyone Else Comes First

One middle-aged woman was dealt a very difficult hand as a young girl of eight. Her father was severely injured in an accident that left him quite helpless, paralyzed. Her mother couldn't cope so she abandoned the family and this little girl had to take care of her father for years during her childhood and young adulthood. She was forced to grow up way too fast and take on immense responsibility. Her childhood was literally taken from her.

The story she created and carried well into her middle age was that she was meant to be the caretaker and:

Everyone else's needs have to be taken care of first. My needs don't matter.

This caretaker mythology carried into her own marriage and family. Everyone else came first. Now she is finally learning to put the past happenings in the past, clearing the way to create her present and future ways of being. She is learning and practicing to put her needs first. She is learning she can live a lighter, more joyous life.

LEAVING YOUR STORY BEHIND

The stories we create around the disturbing patterns of things that happened to us in our early lives can be quite powerful, impacting our lives well into our adulthood, and if unchecked, can follow us to our graves.

There is no reason to carry the stories we created into our future.

I've witnessed the most serious of life's traumas, with the help of a coach, being placed in the past so the person who suffered that trauma can be free of the story surrounding what happened.

Even the trauma of continued sexual abuse as a child can be coached until we can say:

Yes, that happened and it was traumatic at the time, but it is over now and I no longer have to carry the story created around the trauma into my present or future.

Powerful. Freeing.

At one time in our youth we created these stories around the drama or trauma affecting us as part of a way of coping. Once we take a hard look and deconstruct the events, we can move forward with freedom and without constriction or fear.

The Stories You Carry

What is the storyline you carry around about yourself?

What do you tell yourself about yourself?

What story do you present to the world about you?

CHAPTER SIX

What's On Your Lovable List?

WHAT MAKES YOU LOVEABLE?

This is probably the most fun chapter to write. It's a great deal of fun to talk about what makes us loveable in the process of discovering who we are, and changing and transforming our lives. Yet the very idea is often neglected; we're not often asked to think about what makes us loveable, and certainly not asked to talk about it.

For some of us, considering our lovability is a difficult thing to do. We're programmed not to think of all the positives about ourselves. But this is a very important part of the process of figuring out who we are, what we've been, and more importantly, what we want to be as we move forward.

Self-esteem and confidence are so critically important in terms of living a complete, full, purposeful, and joyful life. If we don't have good self-esteem or confidence, we're held back from that. That's what this part of our process is all about.

THE IMPACT OF SOCIALIZATION ON SELF-ESTEEM

An important question is: What blocks us from having that confidence or having that high self-esteem?

There are many answers to that. If you think about it, when we're born, we all start with a clean slate, right?

I like to think all babies are born as *Buddha babies*, nothing but wonder and hope. You are born with a sense of endless possibility. But, in the process of being raised and taught— primarily by parents, but it could be other caregivers—you start to lose that sense of possibility.

Part of raising kids is socialization: giving every kid boundaries and social skills. All of that is incredibly important. I don't mean to minimize that at all. It's an important role of a parent or primary caregiver, but in teaching children about these social skills, we often share some negative things with them, some of the fears that we as parents or caregivers have about the world and ourselves, such as the limitations we learned from our own drama or trauma that were carried along from the past to the present and future.

That bundle of wonder and possibility begins to get chipped away. That's what interferes with the natural kind of self-esteem and confidence that I think every baby is born with.

Sometimes it's blocked; sometimes it's interrupted. It's interrupted purposely. I don't mean purposely by the parents, in terms of setting out to block self-esteem or confidence, but it's the drama, trauma, and challenges of life that happen. Life happens. Things happen. Parents react and respond in the best ways they can, but that drama, trauma, and challenge of life has an effect on how we learn to be in this world.

In addition, many of us are raised—at least in our society, in the United States of America—to not be boastful; to be modest. It's in our socialization genes to tone down this idea of what makes us lovable or what strengths we offer this world.

We're led to be a little too modest about who we are and what makes us shine in this world. That's true of kids, and it happens as we grow older. We hide a lot of our inner charms and minimize our strengths and what makes us really shine. From childhood, we begin to think smaller about ourselves and, sometimes, smaller in terms of what we can accomplish.

It begins to seep in as *scarcity thinking*. We're raised not to be bold, not to scream out to the world what we want, what we want to achieve, how we want to be in this world. At least that's true for a lot of us — maybe not everybody, but a lot of us.

RECLAIMING WHAT MAKES US LOVABLE

That's why this Lovable List concept is important for us, to reclaim or rediscover what really makes us lovable. Think about it right now:

What are the attributes or traits that you have that make you attractive to other people?

What makes people want to be around you?

It's different for everybody, thank goodness. That gives us all the diversity that we see in the world; everybody is uniquely different. But we're attracted to certain people, and certain people are attracted to us based on what I call your Lovable List.

As you look at the drama, the trauma, and how you have responded to that while growing up — how you learned to be and not to be — there will likely be an impact on your self-esteem and your confidence.

How you learned to handle the drama and trauma is all part of the package that teaches you how to be. From that comes your self-esteem and your confidence. It's really important to take a look at this process, and not only the challenges, drama, and trauma you faced — and what you learned from them — but how it resonated with your self-esteem.

The question is, can you rebuild your self-esteem and confidence?

I think you can. But you can only do that when you really take a look at how, specifically in your early life, you got to this point.

How did you learn to be and not to be?

Reflect on what that has done for your confidence level. Once you connect the dots and figure it out you can then decide how you want to be, and exercise your Free Will. You can be the person that you really want to be.

It definitely takes practice to overcome some of the ways of being that you've learned, but you can do it. I've seen it for myself, I've seen it in those that I've worked with, and other people as well.

You can see from what you've read so far that this is not that difficult a process, to break through and make the kinds of changes that we want to make in our lives, but first we have to understand the circumstances, understand the context and how we got to be the way we are. That's the first part of the process.

Now, the fun part starts, when we can choose to look at our shining points.

WHAT'S ON YOUR LOVABLE LIST?

This exercise is simple, but for some people it is going to be harder than for others. Take a piece of paper, and literally write down every single thing you can think about that makes you lovable, that makes people attracted to you. Then, write down more, and write down more, and really push yourself to make an exhaustive list.

Some of these will be things you have never before been able to say out loud. For many of us, we stifle these thoughts and words because we hear a scolding voice in our heads:

You're not supposed to brag.

You're not supposed to gloat.

You're not supposed to tell other people what makes you shine.

This exercise is for allowing yourself to think about these things. Think about what makes you shine to others and write it down. Say it out loud. This can be very, very powerful! It can help us reclaim the ways of being that we gave up long, long ago.

You may have stifled some of these most loveable traits in your past in order to follow the patterns of behavior established by your childhood experiences. Think about this as you read these questions:

Did you learn to stifle your creativity to fit in with your role in the family?

Did you learn to deny your spontaneity because it brought criticism?

Did you, like me, learn to sublimate your own needs and wants?

Were you guided to think of others first, maybe even others only, and deny yourself?

Were you taught to stifle your natural laugh and joy in this world?

Were you raised to follow, rather than lead, even though you're a natural leader?

What loveable parts of yourself are you still hesitant to show?

Whatever your circumstances, whatever you learned to not be, you can now start to reclaim by shining a light. Take a good, hard look at it, and then realize that you're no longer that eight-year-old or twelve-year-old that didn't have much choice in the circumstances of your life. Once we understand, once we've connected the dots, we can then work on making choices.

That's what this exercise is about. It's about fully embracing what makes you lovable. We want to celebrate that. It may be uncomfortable, but it can be really important for making the positive changes in our life that we'd like to make. The purpose of this — like the purpose of so much of what we talk about — is about finding ourselves, our true purpose, and what will bring us joy in life.

What makes you shine?

Without knowing that, how can you know who you really are?

This is important. If you can't look at what makes you a positive, shining, attractive person — the things that make you lovable — then you're not going to be able to purposefully build on the very heart of yourself.

Don't worry if this kind of thinking makes you uncomfortable. Looking at an exhaustive list of what makes us lovable is new and different for most of us. If you're uncomfortable, it can mean that you're facing something significant. Sometimes you have to wade through some unsettling feelings in order to break through an important barrier.

Being uncomfortable is not a bad thing at all, in any part of this process.

Sometimes it means you are on the right track; it means you are *staying with the growing edge.*

I love that phrase. The growing edge is the part of you that is striving to break through what makes us uncomfortable. On the other side of that can be very positive change.

An important step in the process is embracing and celebrating your full Lovable List. If you do this with your full spirit and intentions, it can be extremely powerful. You'll see the possibilities that will materialize when you look at everything that makes you special, wonderful, and lovable in this world.

Do you hear denials and negative statements inside your head when you're reading your list?

This exercise can help you in putting all the past denials, restrictions, judgments, and limitations of self into the past. When they come up in your mind, remember to put them into the past. There's nobody hovering over you, keeping these feelings and wonderful traits inside. There's no reason to hold it in.

Part of creating and living your passion and your joy is releasing everything that's positive about yourself. This Lovable List is a fun part of all of that.

Feel the power of that. Feel the power of *you*, and release it!

Your Lovable List

Write your "Lovable List": all the qualities you have that attract other people to you — *all* your qualities.

CHAPTER SEVEN

Putting Your Past in the Past

IS YOUR PAST HOLDING ON TO YOU?

Much of what we've talked about so far is about exploring, identifying, and getting familiar with the history that we all live, including the challenges, the drama, and the trauma, and how we related to all of these elements in our formative years. We've talked about our behavior patterns and the ways we are guided to be and not to be, in order to navigate our childhood.

Understanding the challenges that you faced and how you responded gives you power. It gives you the power to change, the power to recreate, or the power to create the future that you're looking for. Finding a way to put the past in its place is a vital part of this path.

This chapter is probably the fulcrum, or the turning point of this book. It's the heart of the matter; the essence of all we've been covering and talking about. Everything we've talked about prior to this leads to this, and everything will follow from this: *putting your past in the past.*

Life certainly does happen. Stuff happens. Things happen. Sometimes they're dramatic, sometimes they're traumatic. They happen to us in our early years when we have no control over them. That's the way life is. How we are taught or guided to respond to these things shapes us in the ways that we are and the ways that we learn not to be.

After you put together what has happened to you and how you've responded, you may see it all from a different perspective—maybe for the first time—you can see that the drama or trauma, those things that happened to you, are just that—they were things that *happened*, in *past tense*.

It's really important we understand the past tense nature of all that happened to us.

THE POWER OF THE STORY

Why do we carry that drama and trauma forward into our lives, into our present, and into our future?

Why do we carry that storyline—those stories that we create around all that drama and trauma—when they were simply things that happened, no matter how severe and no matter how powerful?

They simply are things that happened.

Why do we carry them forward?

It has to do with the stories we create to make sense of our experiences. We carry all these memories forward in a mythology that impacts our present and future lives. We carry them around instead of saying:

Okay, that happened. Let me put it in the past and move on.

We end up almost *wearing* the story in carrying it forward. It is vitally important to realize we can't change much in our lives until we face the phenomenon of stories that are created around our experiences in key, early stages of our life.

How do we fix this?

It's like peeling an onion. You begin to expose, layer by layer, what happened in your life, and then you can prioritize.

What are your stories and myths?

What are the real dramas and traumas you experienced?

Beyond the everyday events, what are the patterns that led you to be and act the way you learned to act, in order to navigate and survive?

Once you begin to peel that away and look at it, you can then decide what you are going to do with it. You can say:

Look! I can see these are things that happened, but they're not happening any longer.

PUTTING YOUR PAST IN THE PAST

Example 1: Putting Your Fear of Feeling in the Past

In my own story, as I've already discussed, because of my family dynamics, I learned to stifle my own feelings so that I wouldn't be in danger of hurting my brother. The story I created around that—that restriction and constriction of my full expression of myself—was that my feelings could hurt others, so I learned to keep everything in.

Once I could see how I learned to act that way and deal with my feelings in that way, a whole new area of possibility opened up. Of course, I was only capable of addressing this issue when I could *see* it as something that was part of my *past*. Unfortunately, it took me several decades to really understand it and really put it in its place, but thankfully I was able to do this.

Anybody can do this with their storyline, with the story that they've created around themselves. Once I did that, and put the past in the past, I could then choose to be more expressive, to share my feelings, and to tell people what I wanted and what I needed. After that, much practice was required to undo that storyline and pattern I had adopted.

I would call my experience *drama*. It wasn't traumatic in the sense that it wasn't life and death. It was very significant to me, and shaped my way of being. An example of trauma is living in an abusive family, with physical or sexual abuse against you or against others in your family. Traumatic events can lead to deeper and more troubling stories around those circumstances. In terms of the process, however, the severity is the only difference between trauma and drama. You can see them both as things that happened in that person's life; nothing more, nothing less.

If you physically survive those events, you can put them in the past, even if it's as severe as sexually or physically abusive behavior. It's the stories that you create around that trauma that you carry forward and preserve in the present and future.

I've seen very powerful demonstrations of coaching with people who experienced that kind of severe trauma of abuse, whether it's being raised with alcohol or substance abuse, abandonment, or sexual or physical abuse. In all cases, it is possible to see those events for what they are. They are simply things that happened. Nothing more; nothing less. Once you see that, you can begin to put it in the past.

That is what is so critical for moving forward. If you put those events in the past you can file them away so they no longer exist in the present. Then you can say to yourself:

I am going to create my new way of being because I'm now free of that. It doesn't exist.

Why should I let that past determine how I'm going to act today and tomorrow?

I don't have to do that.

That's what is so exciting about this part of our journey or process together. It's putting it in the past. When you can identify what happened, state strongly to yourself that it happened but it's not happening now, you can say:

I'm going to put this where it belongs: in the past.

When you can put the past where it belongs you can then place the associated stories and myths into the past as well.

This creates a space. For me, once I was no longer running around saying how my feelings will hurt or kill my brother — saying that I have to be careful and guarded and never say what I want or feel — once I put that whole story in the past, it gave me space to try a different way. I began to practice sharing my feelings, being more spontaneous, saying what I need, and connecting with people.

From my own, very personal experience, I discovered how strong the power of connection is to me. It means everything to me, and I lived most of my life denying that, because of the storyline that I had created.

At this point, I can't blame others for that, for what happened in the past. You don't have to either. One does not have to continue that process of blaming others for the circumstances that caused them to be and not be the way they are. Ceasing to blame others is another way you can take control, create a new space to be filled, and begin to implement the positive change that you want in your life. This is where we can finally express Free Will.

Take all the drama and trauma and put it in the past. That's where it belongs. These things are over. They're done. You can choose to freely open up and create a new way of being, by creating that space of possibility and positive change. It's up to you.

You can choose to continue to live that restricted life and blame others for it, or you can say:

That's enough! I understand, I see. I'm going to put that in the past, and I'm going to create the possibilities that will make me happiest and most fulfilled.

The choice is yours.

Here are two further examples of people facing the past, putting it in the past, moving on, and creating new possibilities.

Example 2: Putting Sexual Abuse in the Past

I once attended a group coaching session. Our leader was working with a woman in her mid-thirties. She had volunteered to be a coaching subject for an assembly of people who were going through the group coaching process together.

Many of us had shared our stories, but hers was an extremely moving one. As a witness — as someone who was participating in this program — I was very strongly affected. She was talking, quite openly and emotionally, about how as a young child of about six or seven, and continuing for several years, she was sexually abused by her father. The leader kept asking her questions and I started to get upset. I was moved almost to charge the stage where she was being coached.

It bothered me that the coach, the leader, seemed to be pushing her hard to talk, although she was getting very emotional. To me he seemed too blasé, rather removed from it. He just kept probing and pushing. He never seemed to be taking her any place she didn't want to go, but I kept thinking:

He's not understanding. He's not being sensitive. Why doesn't he just put his arms around this woman and care for her?

There I was in my seat watching this, and I was ready to jump up, to defend her, and argue with the coach, because I thought he wasn't being sensitive to her pain. The opposite was true. He was incredibly in touch with who this person was and what she was expressing, but he also knew that those were events that happened so long ago, she needed to release them, put them back in the past where they belong, and not carry them forward in her life.

Finally I started to understand. He was showing us that he was guiding her simply to *look* at what happened to her. Even as emotional as it was, even though it happened twenty years before in her life, even though it brought up all this pain, he kept asking questions about it.

I began to fully realize—at about the same time that she did; I was right there with her—that what she was talking about happened *in the past*. Yes, it was traumatic. Yes, it was horrific. Yes, it was horrible of her father to do that, but it's over now. When that light of understanding went on in her head, her whole expression changed.

There was an immediate shift in her. I mean it was *immediate*. Her whole expression changed. She was excited and thrilled. You could literally see it in her face; she saw a whole new future for herself.

This young woman was so appreciative, and she expressed it to the coach. She created a new outlook and new possibilities, simply because she was guided to look at what happened in the past in a healthy way. Now that she had the tools to put the past in the proper place, she could proceed to working on exploring herself and, with practice, rediscover the ways that she wants to be, ways that she gave up so long ago.

She realized she had been carrying these stories and this experience around with her for over twenty years. They happened to her but weren't happening anymore. She had survived them physically, and went on and became a fully functioning and mature young woman.

She carried the *story* she had created from the trauma. The leader guided her, in a positive way, to take a look at that traumatic event and see the trauma that happened to her had been over for twenty years. Putting the events in the past now gave her the freedom to change her story.

I'm not going to say that it was magical and she never would have to deal with any of those issues again, but it was clearly a major shift for her. She could, from that point on, put her traumatic past into the past and stop carrying it forward, and begin to practice a new way of being, and moving forward with her life. It was really quite amazing.

Example 3: Putting Joylessness in the Past

Remember the little girl who had the taskmaster for a mother?

I worked with her as a client for a while. As we discussed, her childhood was full of tasks and demands and her mother provided little affection or praise. She described her mother as cold and removed. If she didn't complete her full list of chores, she got the wrath of her mother, not physical abuse, but very stern looks and scolding.

It wasn't until we started talking, and she started her coaching with me, that she was able to look at all of those experiences as in the past. Her mother was not there anymore so she no longer had to satisfy her demands; she no longer had to fear her mother's dissatisfaction over her performance.

That little girl responded to her childhood by becoming responsible and learning to be mature very early. She was a hard worker and this trait persisted into her adulthood. But what she gave up was the freedom of childhood expression, of laughter, of fun, of the choice of doing things or not doing things. She had given up quite a bit. As a young woman, even with children of her own, she was still living that out. She found her life was lacking joy and was not very positive about what she did. She would just work, and work, and work; she was a worker bee.

Once she began to look at this pattern and was able to put the past in the past, she saw that it wasn't her mother making her life joyless; she was now doing it to herself.

Why did she have to do that to herself?

Why did she have to carry that story through into her adult life?

She didn't. Once she put the past into the past, she was able to explore a whole other side of herself and really relish it. A wonderful smile, great sense of humor, and easy laughter surfaced in her. It was really always there, but in a sneaky way, every once in a while. Now she could just be her joyful self!

Yes, she continues to be a hard worker, but she doesn't have to do things for anybody else. She can do them for herself. She's taken new paths in her career and personal life, and it's all for her now. That's what she's practicing, and it can take a lot of practice to overcome those early patterns.

But you can see that it's all very possible to change our stories, in a real way. Once we face into the reality of what we grew up with in terms of the drama and trauma that lead us to be the way we learned to be or not to be, we can free ourselves of that mythology and the storyline that we carry forward. We don't have to carry it. We just don't. We can choose to be free.

Putting Your Past in Your Past

What are the patterns or habits developed from your past that you are carrying to your present and into the future?

CHAPTER EIGHT

Creating
New Possibilities of Being

GET READY FOR NEW POSSIBILITIES

We've spent a lot of time talking about what's affected us to this point. We have been focusing on everything we've lived, everything we've experienced, everybody that's come into our lives, the dramas, the traumas, and how we've responded.

All of that is prelude to this very important endeavor, which is the creation of new possibilities for our lives.

Once we see and begin to understand what has brought us to this point in our lives, of being and not being, of navigating and surviving the drama and trauma, we have an exciting opportunity. We can now create new possibilities of being for ourselves.

When we shine a light on how our lives have been formed, and put in the past all the drama and trauma, we can then decide for ourselves where we want to go.

LETTING GO OF THE STORIES

What keeps drama and trauma in your life and blocks you from living the life you want?

The answer is in the power you give the stories you carry forward. Holding on to the story brings your past into your present and into your future. You can choose to stop that process.

It is in letting go of the story that we can truly begin to take over and direct our Free Will toward making positive changes in our lives; toward being the kind of person we want to be. We can figure out who we are and who we want to be, and transform our lives into the lives that we want. This is a very exciting part of the whole puzzle.

You have seen that these issues form a pattern that can persist over generations. We can stop that pattern once we clear the way.

Can you see your own patterns?

Can you see that by exploring what effect your experiences had on your behavior, reclaiming what you lost, and putting the past in the past, you can find your purpose and what brings you joy?

Once you clear the way, you can create new possibilities, and that's what this is all about. It is about Free Will. It's about setting your mind to reclaiming the ways you want to be.

Think about how powerful that can be for you.

If you are no longer constrained by the past, if you are no longer blocked by the stories that you carry, you can be free. That's what transformation is all about. Once you see the patterns in your life, once you see the story or stories that you created around the experiences of your life, you can begin to write a new story, you can free yourself. You can break out of the box you have been living in and make purposeful choices. It's a wonderful gift you can give to yourself.

PRACTICE AND PATIENCE

The idea of breaking through those habits to create new possibilities is a simple one, once you understand it. However, it is *not* an easy task to accomplish. It requires work. Just like any purposeful change, it requires practice, to be sure.

After all, how many years have you been practicing your current way of being—ten, twenty, thirty years, or more?

All those years of practicing your old ways have made strong habits that are difficult to break. It can take a little time to undo those patterns and create new ways, but it's definitely possible, and very exciting.

First you will need to understand the patterns through which you've learned to act. Then, you'll need to practice noticing them in action in your life:

That's me again, acting judgmental.

After that, you will recognize the old pattern, consider the situation from your new perspective and *choose* the alternative you want.

I realized I was raised to be judgmental. I had to be judgmental to navigate and survive the drama and trauma in my life, but I don't have to choose to be judgmental now and going forward.

You must first catch yourself being in that pattern—being judgmental, or putting yourself last, or taking care of others at your own expense—and that requires being observant of yourself. Once you begin to practice noticing those patterns day by day, you can catch them quickly and say:

Oops, that's me, acting that way that I was raised to be, but I no longer want to be that way. I no longer want to separate myself from other people. That served me in the past, but that doesn't serve me now. The person I want to be as I move forward will make a different choice.

In this way, you can detach yourself from the old behavior, practice a new way, and before you know it, you will be creating new habits of being. That's what creating new possibilities is all about.

It takes a little work, but it's very exciting work because you're literally re-creating yourself the way you truly want to live your life. I've known many people who have made remarkable changes in their lives, reclaiming ways of being that they gave up many years go. We all have that capability. We all can make that kind of change and can grow to lead the life that we really want to lead. We have that choice.

Whatever your pattern was, the first challenge is to look at your past and learn that pattern. We've spent a lot of time talking about that. Second is to catch yourself. Listen for it. Watch. Observe yourself as you're living your life day by day, and see those repeating patterns.

Eventually, you will be able to catch yourself every time, and can start making an adjustment each day as you reach toward a new way of being.

A person who has learned to stifle or suppress their emotion or feelings — their wants or needs — can learn to practice being sensitive. They can practice being fully expressive of how they feel, being open, stating those needs, stating what it is that they want, being spontaneous with their emotions. They can choose to do that, now that the constraints are off. The drama or trauma that happened long, long ago isn't happening now. You have the freedom to be that new person. A powerful transformation can occur.

It won't happen overnight. It takes some time and it takes some practice, but we can achieve those kinds of goals. It's a new way of thinking that you have to get used to. It's a way of thinking about goals and ways that you want to be, ways that you want to live. It takes some awareness about what was and no longer is and then, you have to figure out how you want to be.

You can also begin to reclaim the traits that you had naturally as a young child but lost in the process of coping with crises. This is all part of choosing to be the person you want to be. You can say:

I want to reclaim the lost parts of myself.

I see who I want to be and I have the freedom to be that person.

CHANGING PERSPECTIVE AND PERCEPTION

Dr. Wayne Dyer, a famous personal growth leader who recently passed away, had a great line that I love to quote.

He used to say, "When you change the way you look at things, the things you look at change."

I think that's an incredibly powerful message for all of us to think about. A lot of what we've been talking about, and a lot of what this book is about is changing the way you look at things. In this case, it's changing the way you look at your own life.

You learned to be a certain way as you grew up, but you can look at it in a new way and don't just accept it as:

That's life. That's the way I am. That's the way it has to be.

If we change that perception and look at it a different way, all of a sudden, everything we look at changes! That is a powerful tool on this quest to find yourself, find your true purpose, and find what brings you the most joy in life. Let us all change the way we look at things, and then the things we look at will change. We can transform our lives.

Creating
New Possibilities of Being

What patterns or habits of your past can you give up now and moving forward?

How will giving up these old patterns open up paths of possibility for you?

CHAPTER NINE

What Brings You Joy?

ASKING NEW QUESTIONS ABOUT PURPOSE AND JOY

Many people struggle to find meaning in life. We sense the lack of it in our lives; we understand that something is missing. However, as we struggle, most people never really ask themselves this question:

What is my life purpose?

It is a very important question to ask.

Were you ever asked as a child growing up or as a teenager or young adult, "What is your purpose?"

Many of us were simply not raised to think in terms of *life purpose*. Many of us were raised to think in more limited terms:

What am I suited for?

What can I reasonably expect to do in my life?

We are sometimes directed toward a path by our family traditions:

This path was good enough for your father (or mother), so it's good enough for you.

Our people have always been _____ (fill in the blank with your family business), so that's what you were meant to do.

This kind of scarcity thinking is too often the way we are raised. Too many of us were not taught or expected to think in *abundance* – to think that anything is possible, that we can aspire to anything that fulfills our purpose.

We are encouraged to think in terms of survival, getting work that will pay the bills and simply sustain us financially.

What about our purpose?

What about what will bring us joy?

In many families these core questions are not even raised for consideration. Expectations may be set low and as a result we don't develop the muscle to think in terms of possibility or purpose.

How many people live their lives doing only what they were expected to do?

How many just do whatever they happened upon after schooling, without much thought at all?

How many spend much of their time wondering, dreaming about what they would love to do, but didn't try?

We get locked into circumstances. We move along in our lives using the autopilot created by life experiences, rather than thinking and striving for what could give deeper purpose, meaning, and satisfaction in life. It is no wonder many of us feel boxed-in, without options.

One of the many benefits of exploring the drama or trauma of your life and the ways you learned to be and not to be is that it leads quite naturally to the question of your purpose and joy.

If you add back some of the ways of being that you lost in the effort to cope with the demands of your early life, you will become more complete, more of who you really are at your core. And when you balance your Strong Suits with some of the attributes and ways of being that were stopped in early life, you can more easily identify what may be your true purpose.

You can begin to ask yourself what will bring you joy!

NEW PATTERNS YIELD NEW PERSPECTIVES

When you were living out the stories you created around the drama and trauma of your early life you boxed yourself into a limited life. Carrying your past experiences and the stories you created around them into your present and future keeps you from knowing and living your true purpose.

How can you think and live in abundance if you are only living with your Strong Suits and leaving much of yourself behind?

How can you live your purpose when you are restricting yourself and not allowing all the ways of being to manifest and be part of your life?

Living half of yourself is by definition living in scarcity. When you start purposefully incorporating new patterns of living, new perspectives on life will emerge.

Remember the child raised by alcoholic or drug-dependent parents?

She survived her traumatic childhood by adopting ways of being that allowed her to navigate the perilous events in her household and survive the emotional rollercoaster of a substance abuse family. She developed particular Strong Suits that persisted into adulthood, but also lost ways of being such as youthful joy, spontaneity, and open expression of feelings. She learned to subjugate important parts of herself to survive the erratic environment at home.

With a pattern of survival like that, how could that person find her true purpose or live her joy?

Once we see how the drama or trauma limited our ways of being, we are free then to explore and rediscover the ways of being we learned to stifle or repress in our early years.

Once you distinguish what happened in the past, in early childhood, from your life today, you can put the past in the past – and move on to the future you want to create for yourself. You can then ask yourself:

What is my unique life purpose?

What will bring me joy?

When you become free to express and live your unique way of being you can spend some time happily exploring the answers to these questions. You can begin to find your purpose and live your joy.

The Intersection of Purpose and Joy

Study this image below.

What would you put in the outermost section of each circle?

As you imagine them overlapping and coming together, what do you see is your purpose?

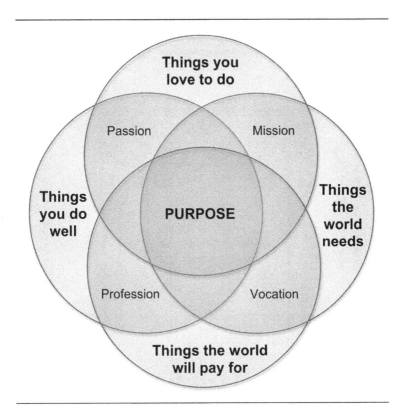

CHAPTER TEN

Practice . . . Practice . . . Practice

MUSCLE MEMORY AND BREAKING PATTERNS

How old are you now?

However old you are, that's how long you've been practicing how you learned to be and not to be. For all of us, that is a significant amount of practice.

As we've been discussing, it's the drama and trauma of your early life that guided you to your ways of being or not being. These patterns of behavior have been practiced over and over, in your childhood and adulthood, whether you intended this or not.

A sports analogy is a good way to take a look at this idea.

Have you ever heard the term *muscle memory*?

Any motion that's repeated and practiced in a sport becomes a muscle memory. If you're a golfer and you've been practicing playing golf, you've been building up a muscle memory of the golf swing. You swing and hit the ball over and over, week after week, until the motion becomes automatic from all that practice.

Living life is the same way. We learn ways of being and ways not to be at an early age. Then we practice those maneuvers over and over, week after week and year after year. That's how we carry our history forward into our present and into our future. It's like a muscle memory of how to be and not to be in life.

You will continue to manage your life by means of this muscle memory until you are able to shine a light on the experiences that formed you. As you have seen, once you explore how you learned to be and not to be, and where your ways of being originated, you can gain the ability to make choices. You can leave your past in the past and reframe your story and your life.

Then you can say:

I want to make some changes in my life. I want to break some patterns.

You can harness Free Will and choose how you want to live the rest of your life.

You can make choices, and you can make positive changes:

Do you want to continue using your Strong Suits, the ways of being you learned to navigate the drama and trauma?

How do you want to build on those Strong Suits?

Are there stories and myths you want to leave behind in the past so you can move forward?

Do you want to reclaim ways of being that you suppressed?

How will you make these changes?

It may seem daunting. Let's look back at the sports analogy.

Suppose you've been practicing your golf swing in the same way for years, but it's not working well for you. You're not able to hit the ball well, and you know something's wrong with your movement. You understand this, but your understanding is not enough to change the swing.

To truly change or transform, you have to do something else, right?

In order to break the habit of the golf swing that's out of kilter, you have to practice new ways. You may have to practice a new grip. You may have to practice changing the plane of the swing. It can help to go to a golf coach who can guide you to make the changes you will need to practice in order to improve your golf swing and game.

In the same way, a life coach can help guide you to gain an understanding of how you've learned to be and not be, and if you wish to change, you will have to practice new ways. We can set goals for practicing new ways of being, and goals for practicing reclaiming those ways of being that we suppressed as a child.

Once you have reached that point of understanding, what comes next?

Now you have to actively work toward your goals in order to truly transform the way you act. At this point, practice will become vitally important; it is only by practicing that you can create all the new possibilities of being that you want in life.

Just like in our golf analogy, understanding the need to change your swing is just the beginning; you will not succeed if you don't work at it. Similarly, if you are a person who learned to suppress spontaneity and free expression of feelings and emotion, you can choose to reclaim those ways of being, but it won't happen without practice.

CREATING A NEW PATTERN

Are you a *yes* person or a *no* person?

When faced with a request or a new situation, do you tend to say *yes* or *no*?

Remember the movie, *Yes Man*, with Jim Carrey? The main character, a very negative person, was taught to practice saying *yes* to everything, no matter what presented itself. The concept made a very funny movie, but it is also interesting how the main character learned from that experience.

I related to that movie very personally, because I experienced the same kind of transformation myself.

A coach I was working with brought to my attention that I had a tendency to be a *no* person, as part of the way I was raised with the drama in my life. I was very careful and cautious. One of the things about being careful is you tend to weigh everything. If anything new presented itself, I had a tendency to say *no*.

The first people who taught me that, by the way, were my two sons.

They used to say, "Dad, we know whenever we come to you with a question, we know we're going to get a *no* right off the bat. If we wait a few beats—maybe half a day or a day—and come back to you with the question, maybe we'll get a *yes*, but the first question will always get a *no*."

Then it was brought to my attention by a coach I was working with at one time.

She said, "Okay, you want to change that? You can change that. Now practice saying yes."

I did what Jim Carrey did in the *Yes Man*. I set a goal and practiced and it worked. I have learned to be much more of a *yes* person and it has added a great deal to my life.

You can reclaim the parts of your ways of being that you learned not to be by first taking a close look at your habits and then making a decision. Then, it becomes a matter of practice.

Even now, although I'm more of a *yes* person than I used to be, it still takes practice and reminders to myself. It's almost like a self-mediation: I try to remind myself to say *yes* instead of *no*.

Not everybody needs to become more of a *yes* person. You could be the opposite. There are people who don't have the inner strength to say *no* to certain situations. They're always saying *yes* and as a result, they may end up feeling taken advantage of, and that they just do too much for other people and put themselves last.

You are more of a *yes* person if, when questions or situations are brought to you, you usually jump in and say *yes*. That can be something with which you want to find a balance. It is possible that you might want to learn how to say *no* more easily. We all need to look at our own unique selves to figure out what ways we want to keep, and which ones we want to change.

PRACTICING NEW WAYS

Once you make a decision that you want something to change, it's all about unlearning old habits and learning new habits. It can be very exciting to begin making changes. We can take on any part of our lives that we have learned to suppress, and we can reclaim those ways of being if we can see them as being positive in our life. That's the way to achieve positive change, and even transformation. We can transform our lives with awareness, dedication, and practice.

Have you ever tried yoga?

If you have, you know it takes practice. Yoga is about training your body in new situations — stretching, elongating muscles, and purposeful relaxation, for example. Practice enables you to become more limber, even if you're a very stiff person. Through yoga practice, you can change quite a bit about your physical being.

In that same way, we can change emotionally, alter our ways of acting, ways of being, and ways of not being. It takes practice. If you get frustrated, try to be patient with yourself and remember that anything worthwhile always takes practice and time.

Once you liberate yourself with the realization that you can choose to change, you can define how you want to be. You can balance your life between your Strong Suits and reclaim some of those ways you learned not to be.

You can set a new path for yourself and clear that space for possibility; the possibility of positive change. Then it is a matter of:

Practice, practice, practice!

This is the beginning of a wonderful and fulfilling journey.

Breaking Old Patterns, Building New Patterns

Identify small steps you can take to break old patterns and practice new ways of being.

Set some small-step goals you can commit to achieving.

Conclusion

Remember Dr. Wayne Dyer's statement, "When you change the way you look at things . . . the things you look at change."

In many ways *Get Out of Your Own Way . . . and Get On With It* is intended to help you change the way you look at things, to change the way you look at your life and how you learned To Be and Not To Be.

The strategies and exercises presented in this book are simple and straightforward, though not always easy. After you study the patterns of your own life and begin to understand your path, you can begin working to transform your life goals.

When you change the way you see the life you led in your formative years, you can begin to change your current patterns of behavior in order to live the life you *choose*, the life you want. You can learn to get out of your own way, to stop carrying forward the patterns of behavior you learned so many years ago.

We each have stories we carry with us, based on dramas and traumas from our childhoods. No matter how severe these issues were, they likely ended many years ago, but still, we carry them with us.

Why do we have to bring all the drama and trauma along with us on our journey?

We don't.

We have the power to put all that history, no matter how painful, in the past where it belongs. Once we change the way we see those patterns in our lives we can stop them and practice new Ways of Being.

Make a commitment to free yourself from the trappings of long-ago learned patterns of behavior. See what happened to you as just that—the things that happened once upon a time, but are now over. There are no limits to the possibilities once you can see this and put these behaviors in the past. Then you can clear the space to create new patterns of behavior and new possibilities.

You can do the exercises and practices provided in this book by yourself. You can also seek support from a life coach or counselor to help you on your path to find your new Ways of Being.

Look forward to finding your life purpose and what will bring you joy. You can do it!

New possibilities of living the life you love await.

Next Steps

Now that you've read my book, I'm sure you're ready to *Get Out of Your Own Way . . . and Get On With It.* To help you with that process it's my pleasure to offer you a *free* coaching session with me, Coach Pete.

It's easy to get started.

Simply send an email to breakthroughwithcoachpete@gmail.com. In the subject line write, "I want to get out of my own way."

Once we have an initial, exploratory conversation by phone to support your decision for coaching with me, I will provide you with your first thirty-minute coaching session, FREE. That's a $60.00 value, just for reading my book.

I look forward to coaching you and supporting you to make the positive changes you seek in your life.

Now, *let's get on with it!*

About the Author

Peter Heymann

Business, Career, and Life Coach

Pete brings to his *Break-Through Career and Life Coaching* practice a diverse background in family counseling, group leadership, sales, marketing, advertising, and business communications.

Pete ran a youth counseling program for five years before applying his people and communications skills to a thirty-year career in sales and marketing. Pete knows business and marketing management from extended real-life experience with corporate and agency services.

During his marketing career, Pete devoted time to a powerful community-based counseling program. For over twelve years he was a highly trained volunteer counselor and then instructor, providing services to people who otherwise could not access counseling. Pete also supplemented his coaching skills through private training, rounding out his experience and developing a system for transforming lives.

In addition to running his career and life coaching practice, Pete is active in community organizing that is directed at issues of social justice and anti-oppression work. He co-facilitates trainings about deconstructing and undoing racism.

Pete brings a unique mixture of experiences to his practice. Besides being a highly trained community counselor and instructor and former manager of a youth counseling center, he is father to two grown sons and a husband of more than forty years. This experience, combined with his corporate marketing and sales proficiency, has given him a rich and diverse set of skills.

Two intensive coaching training experiences have helped shape his coaching philosophy and approach: an intensive twelve-month coaching-to-coach program with intuitive life coach Maura Leon of *Inner Light Coaching* and dynamic training with the *Landmark Worldwide* core curriculum tools for living.

Pete's purpose, mission, and dedication are to provide guidance to people seeking positive change to live the life they love.

heymann.peter@gmail.com

www.breakthroughwithcoachpete.com

Tel: 845.802.0544 | 845.842.1839 cell